MILITARY VEHICLES
COUGARS
BY JOHN HAMILTON

VISIT US AT
WWW.ABDOPUBLISHING.COM

Published by ABDO Publishing Company, 8000 West 78th Street, Suite 310, Edina, MN 55439.

Printed in the United States of America, North Mankato, Minnesota.
072011
092011

Editor: Sue Hamilton
Graphic Design: Sue Hamilton
Cover Design: John Hamilton
Cover Photo: U.S. Army
Interior Photos: AP-pg 11 (insert); Department of Defense-pgs 1-3, 8-11, 14-15, 18-32; Defense Video & Imagery Distribution System-pgs 6-7; Force Protection, Inc.-pgs 12-13, 16-17; United States Marine Corps-pgs 4-5.

Library of Congress Cataloging-in-Publication Data

Hamilton, John, 1959-
   Cougars / John Hamilton.
        p. cm. -- (Military vehicles)
   Includes index.
   ISBN 978-1-61783-075-4
   1. Cougar (Armored military vehicle)--Juvenile literature. I. Title.
   UG446.5.H2834 2012
   623.7'475--dc23

                            2011019735

TABLE OF CONTENTS

★ COUGARS ★

Cougars are medium-weight vehicles used by America's military to transport troops. These tough, reliable vehicles safely move soldiers through many of today's most dangerous battlegrounds.

USMC
G33255

MISSION

Cougars are specially designed to quickly transport combat engineers or infantry squads through areas that might be too dangerous for lighter vehicles to travel, or where the use of heavy vehicles such as tanks would be inappropriate.

XTREME FACT

Cougars are often used as patrol vehicles, bomb disposal vehicles, and to lead convoy missions.

United States soldiers travel in Cougars as part of a security force in Afghanistan in 2009.

COUGAR 4X4 FAST FACTS

Length:	20 feet, 10 inches (6.4 m)
Width:	8 feet, 11 inches (2.7 m)
Height:	9 feet, 11 inches (3 m)
Curb Weight:	17 tons (15.4 metric tons)
Top Speed:	65 miles per hour (105 kph)
Cruising Range:	420 miles (676 km)
Manufacturer:	Force Protection, Inc.
Passengers:	6

A Cougar used as a roadblock in Iraq.

عند الإشارة تقدمو واجتاز بحذر
WHEN SIGNALED PROCEED AND PASS WITH CAUTION

During the War in Iraq, light United States military vehicles such as HMMWVs (Humvees) were very vulnerable to mines and other roadside bombs. These improvised explosive devices (IEDs) tore open the flat bottoms of Humvees, killing and injuring the soldiers inside.

A Humvee (above) follows a 6x6 Cougar (far left) in a 2010 convoy of military vehicles.

Right: A Humvee destroyed by an improvised explosive device (IED) in 2007.

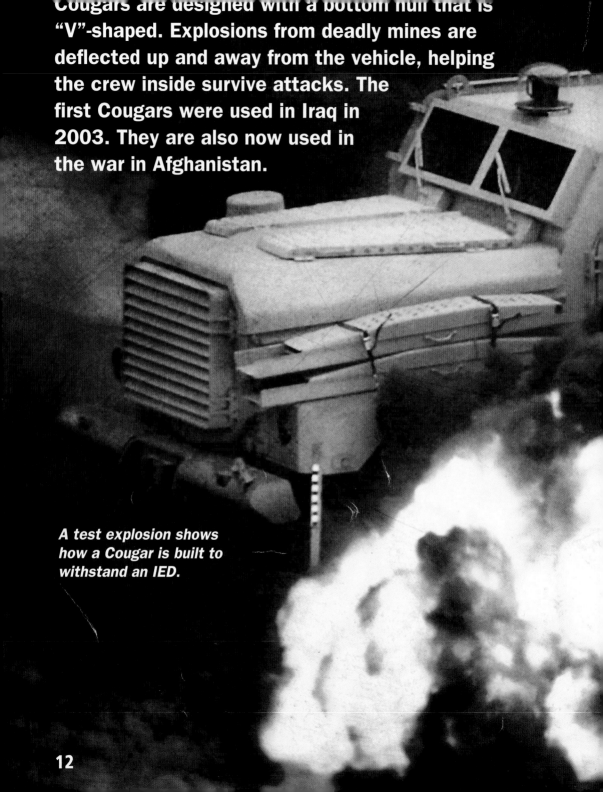

Cougars are designed with a bottom hull that is "V"-shaped. Explosions from deadly mines are deflected up and away from the vehicle, helping the crew inside survive attacks. The first Cougars were used in Iraq in 2003. They are also now used in the war in Afghanistan.

A test explosion shows how a Cougar is built to withstand an IED.

MRAP

Cougars are part of the United States military's MRAP (Mine Resistant Ambush Protected) program. Several companies manufacture MRAP vehicles, which help protect soldiers from hidden mines. Force Protection, Inc. makes the Cougar.

In 2004, the United States Marine Corps reported that no troops had died after more than 300 roadside bomb attacks against Cougars. In the years since, the Cougar has saved the lives of many soldiers.

A Cougar 4x4 follows a soldier as they move through a bazaar in Afghanistan.

VERSIONS

Cougars come in two main versions. The 4x4 Cougar has four wheels. Engine power is transmitted to all four wheels independently (four-wheel drive). The Cougar 4x4 has seating for a driver, co-driver, and four passengers.

The Cougar 6x6 has six wheels. It can carry a driver, co-driver, and up to eight passengers and their equipment.

ENGINE

The Cougar 4x4 is powered by a powerful Caterpillar C7 diesel engine that generates 330 horsepower. It uses an Allison 3500 SP series transmission. The Cougar can run about 420 miles (676 km) on a tank of fuel, with a top speed of approximately 65 miles per hour (105 kph).

Machinists work on a Cougar engine.

19

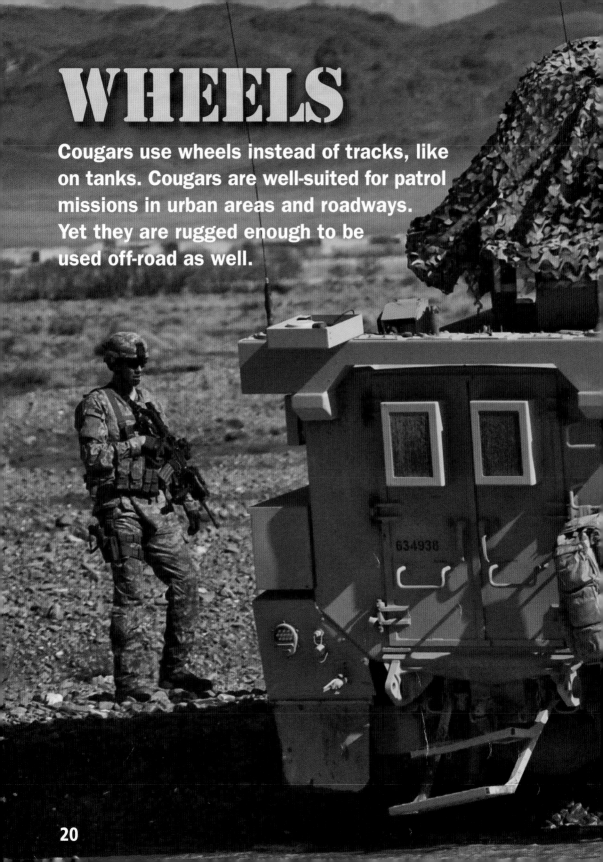

WHEELS

Cougars use wheels instead of tracks, like on tanks. Cougars are well-suited for patrol missions in urban areas and roadways. Yet they are rugged enough to be used off-road as well.

Cougars use "runflat" tires, which can be driven for several miles even when damaged or deflated.

A Cougar transports U.S. security forces across a river and up a muddy bank in Afghanistan.

ARMOR

The exact armor used on Cougars today is classified. Besides their "V"-shaped hulls, Cougars likely protect their occupants with a combination of metals and composite materials such as Kevlar, the same material used in bulletproof vests. Metal cages can also be installed to protect against rocket-propelled grenades. Hardened, bullet-proof glass lets occupants see outside.

Soldiers maneuver a Cougar over a sandy hill in Kuwait. The V-shaped hull, specially designed armor, and bulletproof glass all help protect the people inside the vehicle.

Even if disabled by an
explosion, in many
cases Cougars can
quickly be repaired,
sometimes in
only a few
hours.

US
618737

TP 89

A United States soldier stationed in Iraq prepares to move out in a Cougar to sweep an area for improvised explosive devices (IEDs).

WEAPONS

Cougars use a weapons station mounted on the roof. A single weapon can be mounted, such as an M2 .50-caliber machine gun or an M240 7.62mm machine gun. An Mk 19 automatic grenade launcher can also be mounted.

XTREME FACT

A Cougar's weapon station may either be manned, or operated remotely from inside the vehicle.

A U.S. soldier mans the M2 .50-caliber machine gun in the turret of a Cougar.

The turret of a Cougar.

OPERATORS

In the early days of the War in Iraq, the biggest user of Cougars was the U.S. Marine Corps. Since then, Cougars have been purchased for use by the United States Army, Air Force, and even the Navy. In addition, America's allies have begun using this rugged vehicle, including Canada and the United Kingdom.

Airmen at South Carolina's Charleston Air Force Base load a Cougar 6x6 onto a C-17 Globemaster III for shipment to Iraq.

29

GLOSSARY

ARMOR
A strong, protective covering made to protect military vehicles.

COMBAT ENGINEER
A soldier who specializes in constructing bridges, trenches, bunkers, and other projects under combat conditions. Combat engineers also specialize in destroying enemy fortifications. They also clear land mines so that friendly forces can safely proceed through an area.

CONVOY
A group of vehicles that travel together. In the military, convoys usually have armed escorts to protect them. Cougars are sometimes used in convoys.

DIESEL
A thick petroleum product that is used in diesel engines, such as those found in heavy tanks or trucks.

GRENADE
A bomb with a delayed explosion thrown by hand or shot from a rifle or launcher.

IED

An abbreviation for "improvised explosive device."

INFANTRY

Soldiers who move and fight mainly on foot.

KEVLAR

A light and very strong man-made fiber. It is used to make helmets, vests, and other protective gear for military and law enforcement personnel.

MRAP

An abbreviation for "Mine Resistant Ambush Protected." MRAPs are a family of vehicles designed to withstand roadside bombs and ambushes, mainly in urban areas where the enemy is well hidden. Cougars are MRAPs.

SQUAD

A small unit of soldiers led by a non-commissioned officer such as a sergeant or corporal. The number of soldiers in a squad varies by country. It usually consists of between 8 and 13 soldiers.

TRANSMISSION

A system of gears and other mechanical devices that transfers the power from an engine to the wheels.

INDEX